Michael Harris • David M

WORLD CLASS
LEVEL 1

ACTIVITY BOOK

LONGMAN

LEARNING TO LEARN A

A
Find the words in the title.

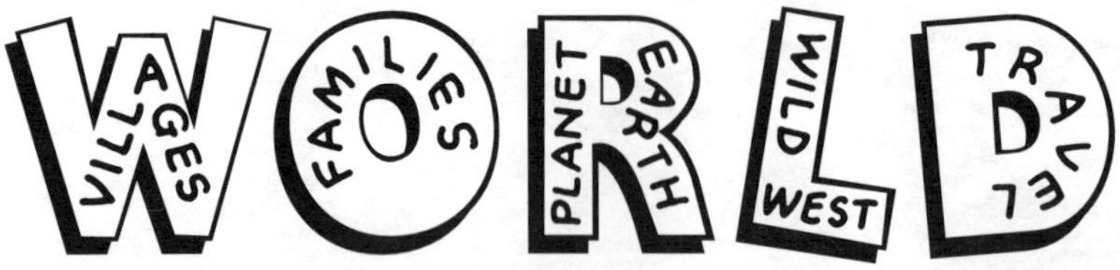

WORLD (VILLAGES, FAMILIES OF, PLANET EARTH, WILD WEST, TRAVEL)

1 Villages 2 ...... 3 ...... 4 ...... 5 ......

CLASS (FUN, STUDENT, TEACHER, LESSON, CASSETTE)

6 ...... 7 ...... 8 ...... 9 ...... 10 ......

B
Activity book quiz. What page are these pictures on?

1 [8]
2 ☐
3 ☐ 
4 ☐
5 ☐
6 ☐

C
Match the symbols with the activities.

1 🖭   a) speaking
2 ✏️   b) listening
3 💬   c) writing

D 🖭
Listen and complete the sentence with these words.

understand / write / listen / answer / match / repeat

1 Answer the questions.
2 .... a book quiz.
3 .... to the story.
4 .... the titles with the pictures.
5 I don't .... 
6 Can you .... that, please?

B

LEARNING TO LEARN

A
Find words in the picture that are similar in your language.
Write the words in your vocabulary book.

B
Write words from the picture in the letters.

A C H S
B M V
R T Z

C
Listening quiz. Listen and guess the objects.

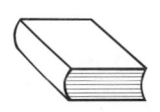

1 rubber   2 ....   3 ....

D
Use the alphabet to find the zebra.

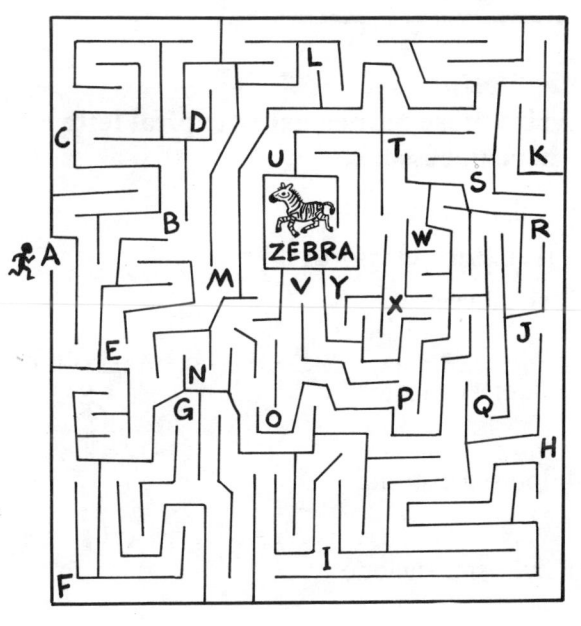

3

LEARNING TO LEARN

A
Complete the form with your information.

WORLD CLASS LEVEL 1

Name .... Age ....

How do you feel about these activities?

Listening to the cassette   Reading

Listening to songs   Writing

Speaking with my partner   Playing games

Key
1 :)
2 :|
3 :(

Punctuation: Names

Herman Munster
George Smith

B
Write these names using capital letters where necessary.

1 william ormond
   William Ormond
2 rita lovelace
   ....
3 daniel cannatella
   ....
4 louis armstrong
   ....
5 sylvester stallone
   ....

C
Listen and write the names of the people.

1 Sam Smith
2 ....
3 ....
4 ....
5 ....
6 ....

D
Find places in this word snake.

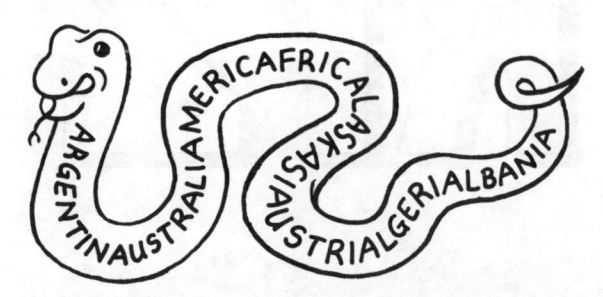

ARGENTINA AUSTRALIA AMERICA AFRICA ALASKA ASIA AUSTRIA ALGERIA ALBANIA

4

MODULE 1
FAMILIES

```
       George — Alice
        (58)    (56)
       doctor  writer
          |
  ┌───────┼────────┬─────────┐
Jackie _ Robert  Alan _ Sarah   Kathy
(34)    (35)    (33)   (33)    (29)
secretary policeman teacher teacher doctor
   |              |
┌──┴──┐           |
Patricia William Debbie
 (11)   (8)      (6)
```

A
Look at the family tree and listen to five members of the family. Write the names.

1 ..Alice........... 4 ....
2 .... 5 ....
3 ....

B
Fill in the gaps. Use the words below.

am / is / isn't / are / aren't / is

1 Kathy and her father ..are... doctors.
2 Debbie .... six years old.
3 Kathy .... married.
4 I .... a secretary. My husband .... a policeman.
5 Sarah and Kathy .... sisters.

Pronunciation
C
Listen and write the sentences. True or false?

1 Robert's thirty-five................ [T]
2 .... [ ]
3 .... [ ]
4 .... [ ]

Punctuation: Capital letters

> **G**iorgos **P**apudopoulos is from **G**reece.

D
Punctuate these sentences.

1 My name is ₿obby ₿rown and ɪ am from ₿ritain.
2 My name is susana sanchez and i am from spain.
3 My name is francois flaubert and i am from france.
4 My name is carl carson and i am from canada.
5 My name is alicia alvarez and i am from argentina.
6 My name is paola pinheiro and i am from portugal.

Spelling corner
E
What are these family words?

1 t h o m r e ..mother......
2 a f t e h r ....
3 r e p n a s t ....
4 r i s t e s ....
5 r a g e d u t h ....

5

2

POLAR BEARS
FACT FILE

- The polar bear is a member of the bear family.

- Polar bears are very big - 800 kg, and up to 3 metres long! Their favourite food is seals.

- They are from the Arctic. It is very cold, but polar bears swim in the Arctic sea!

- Mother polar bears make a house in the snow. The baby bears are with the parents for a year.

A
Read the text above. Then answer the questions.

1 How long are polar bears?
   Three metres.
2 What is their favourite food?
   ....
3 Where are they from?
   ....
4 Is it warm in the Arctic?
   ....
5 How long are baby bears with their parents?
   ....

B
Make questions from the words below and the verb *to be*.

1 How old / you?
   How old are you?   [b]
2 When / your birthday?
   .... [ ]
3 Where / you from?
   .... [ ]
4 What / your favourite animals?
   .... [ ]
5 What / your phone number?
   .... [ ]

Now match the questions with these answers.
a) London   b) twelve   c) 268 3452
d) 21st March   e) cats and dogs

Language extra: a/an

| **an** apple | **an** animal |
| **a** banana | **a** penguin |

C
Look at the rule. Write *a* or *an*.

1 *a* tiger   4 .... big monster
2 .... parrot   5 .... enormous animal
3 .... elephant

D
Circle the odd-one-out.

1 lion (seal) panther tiger
2 wife mother brother sister
3 big black white yellow
4 Herman Lily Eddie Susan

6

3

A
Listen to Frances. What things has she got? Put ✓ or ✗ in the boxes.

1 A pet ✓
2 A bicycle ☐
3 A computer game ☐
4 An English book ☐
5 An English cassette ☐

B
Write sentences about Frances.

1 (a pet)
   She has got a pet.
2 (a bicycle)
   ....
3 (a computer game)
   ....
4 (an English book)
   ....
5 (an English cassette)
   ....

C
Now write sentences about yourself.

1 (a pet)
   I ....
2 (a bicycle)
   ....
3 (a computer game)
   ....
4 (an English book)
   ....
5 (an English cassette)
   ....

Punctuation: Full stops and capital letters

polar bears are very big their favourite food is the seal
Polar bears are very big. Their favourite food is the seal.

D
Write these sentences with capital letters and full stops.

1 he is eleven years old his name is Jabu
   He is eleven years old.
   His name is Jabu.
2 he lives in a village it is in Nepal
   ....
   ....
3 his father is a farmer he hasn't got a tractor
   ....
   ....
4 the family is not rich they have got a small house it hasn't got electricity
   ....
   ....

E
Match the children and their favourite things.

Nikos   Laura   Brahim   Claudia
computer ....
game..   ....

7

4

A

Look at the picture for one minute. Then cover the picture and answer the questions.

1 Have they got a car?
   Yes, they have.

2 Has the mother got matches?
   ....

3 Has the father got a book?
   ....

4 Has the dog got a bone?
   ....

5 Has the boy got a knife?
   ....

6 Has the girl got an apple?
   ....

7 Have they got a cat?
   ....

B

Write questions to make a *Room Survey*.

1 your room/got/a big window?
   Has your room got a big window?

2 you/got/a computer?
   ....

3 your room/got/posters on the wall?
   ....

4 you/got/a radio?
   ....

5 you/got/a video?
   ....

C

Now answer the room survey for yourself in your notebook.

Language extra: Plurals

| book – books | church – churches |
| country – countries | knife – knives |

D

Look at the rule above. Write the words below in the plural in the correct group. You can use the mini-dictionary.

family / sister / baby / match / wolf / bottle / wife / watch

Group 1   **Group 2**
   -s   -es
sisters   ....

....

Group 3   **Group 4**
   -ies   -ves
families   ....

....

5

A

Complete the first text about Norman Normal with these words.

her / his / my / our / she / their / we

1 My name is Norman Normal. ¹...*my*.... wife is called Nancy and ²............. have got two children. ³............. names are Nicholas and Natalie. Nicholas, ⁴............. son, is tall and thin and ⁵............. hair is short and dark. Natalie, our daughter, is also tall and thin and ⁶............. hair is short and dark. ⁷............. has got two pets. Our house is not very big and not very small. We have got a small car.

2 My name is Nancy. I'm 35 years old. My eyes are big and my hair is long and blonde.

3 My name is Nicholas. I'm 13. I haven't got a pet. My favourite thing is my computer.

4 My name is Natalie. I'm 11. I've got a pet dog called Rex and a hamster called Hattie.

B

Match the texts with the pictures.

C

True or false?

1 The Normal Family has got three pets. ☐

2 Nancy has got dark hair. ☐

3 Their house is not very big. ☐

Pronunciation: is/has

She's big. = She **is** big.
She's got a car. = She **has** got a car.

D

Listen to the sentences. *Is* or *has*?

1 ...*is*.... 3 .... 5 ....

2 .... 4 ....

Language extra: Word order

She's got a **car red**. ✗
She's got a **red car**. ✓

E

Correct the sentences if necessary.

1 It's an animal enormous.
   It's *an enormous animal*..........

2 They've got a house very small.
   ....

3 He's got an old car.
   ....

4 His sport favourite is badminton.
   ....

6

A

Read the story about The Silly Family. True or false?

1 The Sillies have got their pets with them. [T]
2 Horace has got black glasses. ☐
3 Horace has got a map. ☐
4 A policeman is in the jungle. ☐
5 The snake has got a good idea. ☐
6 They are all happy at the end. ☐

2 Later . . .
?
It's okay. I've got a map.
3
Where is Rudolf?
6
Where's Darlene?
7
8 Then . . .
I've got an idea.
11
Your pets aren't free.
And our Rudolf and Darlene aren't free!
12 The solution to the problem.
Bye!
Bye, Maggie!
Bye!

7

Language revision
A
One sentence is correct. Correct the others.

1 We no have got a big garden.

   We haven't got a big garden.

   ....

2 My favourite animals is tigers.

   ....

   ....

3 He's name is Tom.

   ....

   ....

4 I am not tall.

   ....

   ....

5 His nose are long and thin.

   ....

   ....

6 I'm have a brother and a sister.

   ....

   ....

7 She name is Janet.

   ....

   ....

8 The farmer haven't got a tractor.

   ....

   ....

Useful vocabulary
B
Here are some important words from Module 1. Write them in your vocabulary book.

blonde / brother / cupboard / dark / duck / elephant / fantastic / father / favourite / fire / garden / grandmother / hen / lion / mother / tall / sister / table / tiger / window

Now write the words in the correct box

Family	*brother* ....
	....
	....
	....
	....
Animals	....
	....
	....
	....
	....
Adjectives	*dark* ....
	....
	....
	....
	....
House	....
	....
	....
	....
	....

C

Now put these words in alphabetical order. Check your answers in the mini-dictionary.

parents ☐ parrot ☐ penguin ☐
polar bear ☐ panther [1] pet ☐
pig ☐ plate ☐

Pronunciation

D

Listen and write letters in boxes 1 to 12.

1	2	3	4	5	6
7	8	9	10	11	12

G	I	O	O	F	U
E	R	N	N	I	C
R	A	D	A	R	K
G	H	E	N	E	C

Now find eight words from exercise B in the word square.

Dr Grammar

E

Correct the sentences.

1 My brother he is thin.
   My brother is thin.

2 His parents they have got a big car.
   ....

3 The lion it is from Africa.
   ....

4 Tom Cruise he is famous.
   ....

5 Carolina she is from a rich family.
   ....

Spelling corner: er

F

Look at the pictures. What are the words?

1 ☐ ☐ ☐ E R
2 ☐ ☐ ☐ E R
3 ☐ ☐ ☐ ☐ ☐ E R
4 ☐ ☐ ☐ E R ☐
5 ☐ ☐ ☐ E R

Extra time!

G

Colour the picture. What animal is it?

1 = red   4 = yellow
2 = blue   5 = brown
3 = green   6 = black

It is a ....

MODULE 2
FUN 8

A
Put the verbs in brackets in the correct form.

My hobby   Damian Delaney

My hobby is making models. I (not make)
¹ _don't make_ model aeroplanes or cars, I (make)
² _____ model ships. My dad (go) ³ _____ to
different countries and he (get) ⁴ _____ models
for me.
    I (make) ⁵ _____ the models in my room. I
(not play) ⁶ _____ with them, I (collect)
⁷ _____ them. Now I've got ten models. My
favourite is a small model of the Pinta,
Columbus' ship.
    The only problem is my little brother Tommy.
He (not understand) ⁸ _____ and he
(want) ⁹ _____ to play with the ships. We
(not give) ¹⁰ _____ him the models!

B
Put these sentences about Damian in the negative.

1 Damian makes model aeroplanes.
   Damian does not make model aeroplanes.

2 His dad gives him national dolls.

   ....

3 Damian makes models in the garden.

   ....

4 His brother plays with models.

   ....

C
Write four sentences about your and your friend's hobbies in your notebook.

Maria collects badges.

D 🎧
Listen to these plurals.

Group 1:   books
Group 2:   coins
Group 3:   badges

Listen and put these words in the correct group.

stamps [1]   comics [ ]
boxes [ ]   dolls [ ]
models [ ]   games [ ]

E
Match the sports with the pictures.

tennis / badminton / football / hockey

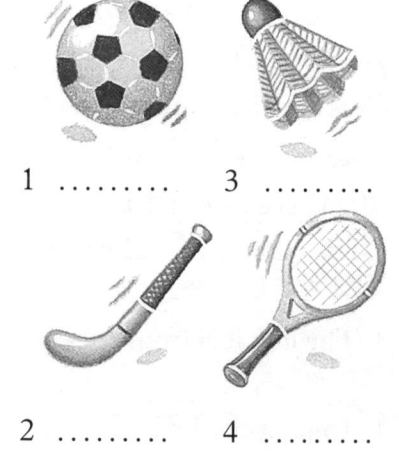

1 ....   3 ....

2 ....   4 ....

14

9

A
Write about these pictures.

1 ....
2 ....
3 ....
4 ....
5 ....
6 ....

B
Write three sentences about the games people in your family like.

1 My sister likes cards.
2 ....
3 ....
4 ....

Language extra: Irregular plurals

people	children
men	women
oxen	

C
Match the plurals in the box with the singulars below.

1 child *children*
2 person ....
3 man ....
4 ox ....
5 woman ....

D
Listen to these words from exercise C. Singular (S) or plural (P)?

1 [S]   3 [ ]   5 [ ]
2 [ ]   4 [ ]   6 [ ]

15

10

A
Listen to Sophie and Jason. What can they do? Complete the table.

	Sophie	Jason
swim	✓	✗
ride a bicycle		
ride a horse		
ski		
climb		

B
Write questions and short answers about Sophie and Jason. Use *can* and *can't*.

1 (Sophie / swim) Can Sophie swim?
Yes, she can.

2 (Jason / ski) ....
....

3 (Sophie / ride a horse) ....
....

4 (Jason / ride a bicycle) ....
....

C
Write three sentences in your notebook about what your family *can* and *can't* do.

1 My mum can ride a bicycle but she can't ski.

D
Match these words with the verbs in the pictures.

tennis / a horse / comics / television / films / football / videos / a bicycle / stories / a unicycle / computer games / books

PLAY — football, tennis, computer games

WATCH

RIDE

READ

16

11

A
Complete the dialogue.

JASON: (like)¹ Do you like .... parties, Alice?

ALICE: No, I hate them.

JASON: And your sister, Karen. (like) ² .... them?

ALICE: Yes, she loves parties.

JASON: Oh? (like)³ .... dancing?
ALICE: Yes, she does.

JASON: What music (like)⁴ .... ?
ALICE: She likes Prince.

JASON: And who (Karen go)⁵ .... to parties with?

ALICE: Look Jason. I don't know. Ask her!

Now listen and check your answers.

B
Use these words to write questions.

1 do / go / you / to parties?
   Do you go to parties?

2 dance / your sister / at parties? / does
   ....

3 party games? / like / you / do
   ....

4 music / your brother / like? / does / what
   ....

5 dance with? / you / who / do
   ....

6 to parties? / your friends / do / go
   ....

Language extra: Question words

> **What** do you do at parties?
> **Who** do you dance with?
> **Where** do you come from?

C
Use the words in the picture to write questions in your notebook.

What games do you like?

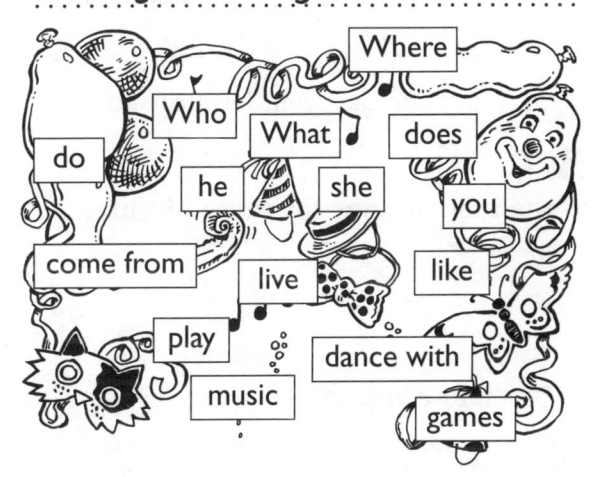

(picture contains words: Where, Who, What, does, do, he, she, you, come from, live, like, play, music, dance with, games)

Punctuation: Question marks

> Where do you come from**?**

D
Punctuate these questions.

1 Where do you live?
2 does your brother like parties
3 what music does he like
4 who do you dance with

E
Listen to the questions from exercise D and mark the intonation.

17

12

A
Listen and complete the instructions.

1 In pairs, ¹....*match*... the instructions with the pictures. ²..............
   ³.............. in your book. Then ⁴.............. and ⁵.............. your answers.

2 ¹.................. at the pictures and ².................. your hobbies. In groups, ³............ your list. ⁴........ the class your favourite hobbies.

B
Write instructions for these pictures.

(use)   (write)

1 *Don't use a pen. Use a pencil.*   4 ....

(open)   (look at)

2 ....   5 ....

(pick up)

3 ....

Language extra: Numbers
C
Write the numbers next to the words.

one [1]   two [ ]   three [ ]   four [ ]
five [ ]   six [ ]   seven [ ]   eight [ ]
nine [ ]   ten [ ]   eleven [ ]   twelve [ ]
thirteen [ ]   fourteen [ ]   fifteen [ ]
sixteen [ ]   seventeen [ ]   eighteen [ ]
nineteen [ ]   twenty [ ]   twenty-one [ ]
twenty-five [ ]   thirty-one [ ]
forty-three [ ]   fifty-five [ ]   sixty [ ]

D
Do the sums and then write the numbers.

1 11 − 8 = *three*
2 50 + 20 = ...
3 19 − 7 = ...
4 22 × 2 = ...
5 42 + 17 = ...

Spelling corner: Numbers
E
Correct the spelling.

1 (12) twelf   3 (2) too
   twelve   ....

2 (14) forteen   4 (40) fourty
   ....

18

13

A
Listen and write the name of the sport.

tennis / football / table tennis /
swimming / golf

1 ..golf........   4 ....
2 ....   5 ....
3 ....

B
Listen to the song. Match the verses (1 to 5) with the pictures (A to E).

A.
B.
C.
D.
E.

C
Listen to the song again. Sing it and do the things.

If you're happy and you know it
Clap your hands
If you're happy and you know it
Clap your hands
If you're happy and you know it
And you really want to show it
If you're happy and you know it
Clap your hands

D
Number code. A is 1, B is 2, C is 3, etc. What are these sentences?

1 8 5 12 12 15   13 25   14 1 13 5   9 19
   H E L L O   M Y   N A M E   I S
   10 21 4 25
   J U D Y

2 9 1 13   6 18 15 13   12 15 14 4 15 14
   .. ..

3 9   12 9 11 5   3 15 13 16 21 20 5 18
   .. ..
   7 1 13 5 19
   ....

4 9   3 1 14   16 12 1 25   20 5 14 14 9 19
   .. ..
   1 14 4   9   3 1 14   19 23 9 13
   ....

19

13

E
Bill and Ben are brothers. Find five differences between them.

1 <u>Bill likes dominoes. Ben doesn't.</u>
2 ....
3 ....
4 ....
5 ....

F
Complete the sentences below and fill in the puzzle. Then find the word.

1 Parties are great! They are f _antastic_..
2 I like board g ....
3 My sister is a real party person. She l .... parties.
4 A game with numbers. d ....
5 She likes c .... games with blocks.
6 At p .... you can dance and play games.
7 Computer games are not bad for c .... They are just good fun.
8 My sister w .... films on televison.
9 Do you want to have a game of t ....?

					5			
		3		6	7	8	
	2		4				9
¹F							
A							
N							
T							
A							
S							
T							
I							
C							

20

14

Language revision

A
Use the table to write five sentences about Sally.

Likes	
Doesn't like	
Hobbies	
Sports	
Languages	ESPAÑOL
School subjects	English ☹ Spanish ☺

1 Sally likes dominoes.

2 ....

3 ....

4 ....

5 ....

6 ....

B
Use these words to write sentences about Sally.

1 (like / television?)
Does she like television?

2 (what / hobbies / do?)
....

3 (can / play / tennis?)
....

4 (what languages / study?)
....

5 (like / Spanish?)
....

6 (like / computer games?)
....

7 (can / play / football?)
....

21

14

Useful vocabulary

C
Here are some important words from Module 2. Check they are in your vocabulary book.

hobbies / make / collect / read / watch / like / games / models / dolls / stamps / coin / football / tennis / chess / dominoes / computer games / board games / walk / ride / carry / play / dance / parties / go / pick up / show / hold / look at

Look at the words again. Which are nouns, which are verbs and which can be both?

Nouns	Verbs
games	make

Dr Grammar

D
Correct these questions.

1 You like football?
   Do you like football?

2 What hobbies he do?
   ....

3 Your sister collect stamps?
   ....

4 Where he make his models?
   ....

5 They watch television?
   ....

6 You dance at parties?
   ....

Spelling corner: al/el/il/le

animal   model   pencil   table

E
Listen and write the words you hear.

1 *example*
2 ....
3 ....
4 ....
5 ....

MODULE 3
VILLAGES 15

A
Write sentences using *there is/isn't* and *there are/aren't*.

1 (church)
   There isn't a church.

2 (shops)
   There are three shops.

3 (banks)
   ....

4 (a school)
   ....

5 (a restaurant)
   ....

6 (a cinema)
   ....

7 (a factory)
   ....

8 (a toy shop)
   ....

B
Write questions in your notebook. Then write answers about where *you* live. Use the words in exercise A.

C
What are these places?

1 kanb   bank
2 shocol   ....
3 necaim   ....
4 cofraty   ....
5 opsh   ....

Pronunciation: the letter 'o'

D
Say the words and put them in the correct group.

shop / old / mosque / doctor's / video / olive / local

Group 1	Group 2
shop	old
....	....
....	....
....	

Now listen and check your answers. Repeat the words.

23

16

A

Look at the picture below. Write questions and short answers about the things in the shop.

1 (cassettes)
   Are there any cassettes?
   Yes, there are.

2 (ice cream)
   Is there any ice-cream?
   No, there isn't.

3 (crisps)

   ....

   ....

4 (chocolate)

   ....

   ....

5 (drinks)

   ....

   ....

6 (computer games)

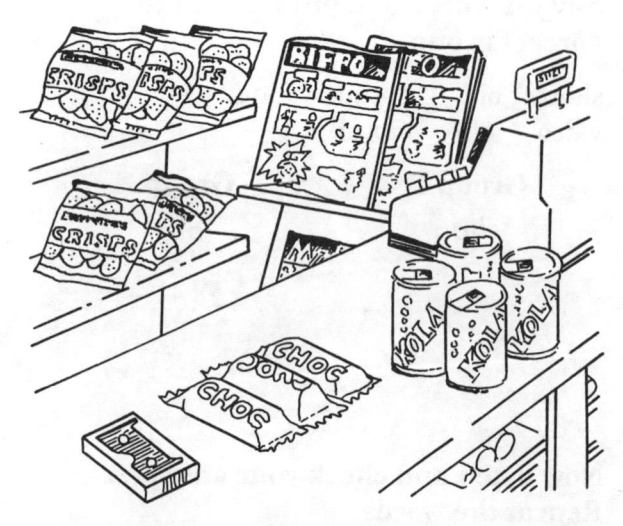

   ....

   ....

Language extra: Prices

£1.50 = one pound fifty
85p = eighty-five pence

B

Look at the shopping list. Write the prices in full.

crisps	75p	seventy-five pence.
drinks	£1.20	....
sweets	40p	....
comics	£1.65	....
TOTAL	£4.00	....

C

Put the things in the correct column. You can use the mini-dictionary. Add two more words to each column.

apples / carrots / ice cream / potatoes / sweets / bananas / rice / cakes / oranges

Fruit	Vegetables	Others
....	....	....
....	....	....
....	....	....
....	....	....

17

A
Listen to Jessica and Peter. Complete the table.

	Jessica	Peter
Country		
Favourite lesson		
Interest		

B
Change the words in *italics* and rewrite the sentences. Use the words below:

they / them / he / she / it / him / her

1 *Jessica* likes *school*.
   She likes it.

2 *Peter* doesn't like *lessons*.
   ....

3 What lessons do *Jessica and Peter* like?
   ....

4 I listen to music with *my sister*.
   ....

5 I play computer games with *my brother*.
   ....

C
Write sentences about *you*.

1 What is your favourite lesson?
   ....

2 Who is your favourite teacher?
   ....

3 What is your hobby or interest?
   ....

4 What music do you like?
   ....

5 What sports do you play?
   ....

6 What sweets do you buy?
   ....

Spelling corner: oo

D
Write words below the clues.

1 You learn here.
   ☐ ☐ ☐ o o ☐

2 You can swim here.
   ☐ o o ☐

3 You have lessons here.
   ☐ ☐ ☐ ☐ ☐ ☐ o o ☐

4 You eat this.
   ☐ o o ☐

5 You see it in the sky at night.
   ☐ o o ☐

25

18

A
Listen and look at the pictures. Are the things Brian's or Lucy's?

1 Brian's
2 ....
3 ....
4 ....
5 ....
6 ....

B
Complete the sentences with these words:

ours / his / mine / hers / theirs

1 LUCY: The dolls are *mine*.
2 BRIAN: The cat is ....
3 LUCY: The dog is ....
4 MOTHER: The pets are ....
5 BRIAN AND LUCY: The bicycles are ....

Punctuation: Apostrophes

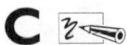

C
Put apostrophes, where necessary, in these sentences.

1 Brian's bicycle is black.
2 The dolls are Lucys.
3 The stamps are yours.
4 Lucys cat is called Tammie.
5 The childrens bicycles are new.

Language extra: Greetings

Hi!
Good morning.

D
Complete these sentences with the greetings.

.... Miss Thacker.

.... Paul!

.... Laura!

Now listen and check your answers.

Which greeting is very friendly?
....
Which greeting is polite?
....

E
Match the jobs with the definitions.

1 A doctor — a) works in a school.
2 A teacher — b) serves you drinks and food.
3 A waiter — c) looks after your teeth.
4 A dentist — d) gives you medicine.

26

19

A

Look at the school festival. What can you see? Complete the sentences with the correct form of the verb in brackets.

1 People *are eating* sweets and cakes. (eat)

2 The children .... school uniform. (not wear)

3 It's a nice day.
  It .... (not rain)

4 Some parents .... in a race. (run)

5 My sister .... with her friend. (dance)

Punctuation: Name and address

B

Look at the commas and full stop in this address.

Cris Warren,

15 Market Street,

Middleton,

United Kingdom.

Now write your own name and address on this postcard.

Language extra: Ordinal numbers

first, second, third, fourth, fifth

C

Write words fom the box in the spaces.

3rd *third*   5th ....

1st ....   4th ....

2nd ....

Now check your answers on page 104 of the Students' Book.

20

A
Read and listen to the story. Answer these questions.

1 Whose idea is it to play with the dinosaur?

....
....

2 Where do the children go?

....

3 Who do they see there?

....
....

4 Where does she go, when she sees the dinosaur?

....
....

5 Who does she talk to?

....
....

6 What does he do when he sees the dinosaur?

....
....

7 Who telephones the police?

....
....

8 What do the police do?

....
....

9 What do the children write on the blackboard?

....

1 Fantastic! It's the first day of the holidays! What do you want to do?

We can play with my model aeroplanes.

I don't like model aeroplanes. But I've got an idea!

4 HELP!!!!

5 Mr Boggis!! In the park there's a dinosaur!!! Go to the park!

A dinosaur? In Tiddlehampto There aren't any dinosaurs h

8 Is that the police? Doris? It's terrible. There are enormous dinosaurs in the park in Tiddlehampton.

Don't worry! We're coming!

9

Help!! A dinosaur!
Don't worry Phil. It isn't real.
That's great Annie!
DINOSAUR
That's Mrs Stott, our teacher!
Good morning children. What are you doing?
HELP!!! It's true. It's a monster!! It's attacking me!
Captain! Can you help us? There's an enormous dinosaur in the park!!
A dinosaur? No problems. Wait a moment. I have an idea!

21

Language revision
A
Correct these sentences.

1 There is two restaurants in the street.
   There are two restaurants in the street.

2 The books are mines.
   ....

3 She playing tennis at the moment.
   ....

4 There's a cinema in your village?
   ....

5 Our's house has got a small garden.
   ....

6 It no raining now.
   ....

Useful vocabulary
B LEARN TO LEARN
What are these words in your language? Write the words in your vocabulary book. Are they similar in your language?

dentist	crisps
sweets	park
waiter	policewoman
shop	doctor
factory	chocolate
bank	cakes
cinema	ice cream

C
Put the words from exercise B in the correct circle.

Jobs

Food/Drink

Places

Dr Grammar

> He watching TV. ✗
> He's watching TV. ✓   He is watching TV. ✓

D
Complete these sentences with *am/are/is*.

1 They ....*are*.... playing computer games.
2 She .... watching a video.
3 You .... not listening to me!
4 I .... doing my homework now.
5 He................ making a model car.

Spelling corner: double letter + *ing*

E
Complete the sentences below with the verbs in the correct form.

swim / get / run / sit / put / win

1 She is .*getting*............ her books off the shelf.
2 He is .... in a comfortable chair.
3 They are .... in the river.
4 She is .... the race.
5 He is .... his things in his bag.
6 She is .... very fast.

Extra time!

F
Write questions for these answers.

1 **Question 1**
What is your favourite colour?
Question 2
What colour is your book?
Question 3
What colour are tomatoes?
Answer: Red

2 **Question 1**
....
Question 2
....
Question 3
....
Answer: England

3 **Question 1**
....
Question 2
....
Question 3
....
Answer: Because I'm cold.

MODULE 4
THE WILD WEST
22

A
Read about the Mohawk Indians. Put the words in brackets in the past tense.

The Mohawk Indians (not live) ¹ _didn't live_ on the plains of America. They (live) ² .... in the woods of Canada and the north of the United States.

They (not travel) ³ .... They lived in villages. They (not have) ⁴ .... horses, they (walk) ⁵ .... or (travel) ⁶ .... by canoe on the rivers. They (not hunt) ⁷ .... buffaloes. They (hunt) ⁸ .... bears and other animals. They (use) ⁹ .... the skins for clothes and the bones for knives and arrows. They (not have) ¹⁰ .... tents, but they lived in big houses.

Spelling corner
B
Write the past tense of these verbs.

help	_helped_	travel	....
arrive	....	carry	....
cook	....	study	....
talk	....	play	....
walk	....		

Which three verbs are irregular?

C
In your notebook, write three sentences about what your family did and did not do yesterday. Use the verbs in exercise B.

1 _My brother played tennis._
2 _My mum didn't walk to work._

Pronunciation
D
Listen and repeat these verbs.

Group 1	Group 2	Group 3
played	_cooked_	_carried_
....	....	....
....	....	....
....	....	....

Now listen and write these verbs in the correct group.

studied / talked / walked / arrived / liked / helped / travelled

23

A
Read about cowboys and match the drawings with the paragraphs.

1. Cowboys travelled thousands of miles with their cows. They started in Texas and arrived in the railway towns. The trains then carried the cows to the East of the United States.

2. The cows needed twenty gallons (about a hundred litres) of water a day. Many of the cows died before they arrived.

3. When the cowboys arrived in the towns, they went to the barber's to get a haircut and then they went to the saloon. Wild west towns were violent and had gunmen like Billy the Kid. A famous sheriff was Wyatt Earp, sheriff of Dodge City.

Language extra: Why/because

Why do you go to the barber's?
Because you want a haircut.

B
Match the questions and answers.

1. Why do you go to the bank? [e]
2. Why do you go to the cinema? [ ]
3. Why do you go to the discotheque? [ ]
4. Why do you go to the supermarket? [ ]
5. Why do you go to a railway station? [ ]

a) Because you want to catch a train.
b) Because you want to dance.
c) Because you want to buy some food.
d) Because you want to watch a film.
e) Because you want to get some money.

C
Write directions to go from your school to one of the places below in your notebook.

a hotel / a park / a cinema / a bank / a restaurant

Go out of the school. Turn left. Turn right at the first street. Then, go straight on. The hotel is on the right.

D
Classify the words below into Wild West town (W), Modern town (M) or both (B).

railway station [B]   barber's [ ]   cinema [ ]
disco [ ]   sheriff's office [ ]   bank [ ]
supermarket [ ]   stables [ ]   hotel [ ]
saloon [ ]   garage [ ]   factory [ ]

33

24

A

Look at the picture of Laura's house. Find six things that are wrong and write sentences in your notebook.

1 *In Laura's house there wasn't a washing machine.*

Punctuation: Commas in lists

> Wolves, bears, wild cats **and** other animals lived in the big woods.

B

Use the words below and commas to write sentences about Laura's house.

1 In the house: attic/small bedroom/big room

   In the house there was an attic, a small bedroom and a big room.

2 In the big room: cooker/cupboard/a big table/a rocking chair/a fire

3 In the cupboard: some plates/some knives/some forks/some bottles

Language extra: Time

> 8.00 a.m. = 8 o'clock in the morning
> 4.00 p.m. = 4 o'clock in the afternoon

C

Listen to the dialogue between Sam and his teacher. Complete the table.

3 o'clock	at school
5 o'clock	
6 o'clock	
7 o'clock	
9 o'clock	

D

Write sentences in your notebook about where you were on Monday. Use the times below.

6.00 a.m. / 8.00 a.m. / 11 p.m. / 6 p.m. / 11.00 a.m.

At six o'clock I was in bed.

34

25

A
Listen to a quiz show about The Wild West. Decide if the statements are true or false.

1 *False*.......... 4 ....
2 .... 5 ....
3 ....

Language extra: Question words

> **Which** programmes are westerns?
> *High Noon* and *Little House*.
> **What** programmes do you like?
> I like cartoons.
> **When** is *High Noon* on TV?
> At 8 o'clock.
> **Where** is Laura's house?
> In the woods.
> **Who** is in *Comedy Classsics* this week?
> Charlie Chaplin.

B
Complete the questions with question words from the box above.

1 *Which* .... programmes do you want to watch?
2 .... programmes are cartoons?
3 .... do John and Peter live?
4 .... do you watch television?
5 .... is on The Rock Show this week?
6 .... programmes do you like?

C
Match the words below with the television programmes.

comedy programmes / sports programmes / westerns / nature programmes / cartoons / quiz shows

1  .... 4 ....
2  .... 5 .... 
3  .... 6 .... 

D
Write sentences in your notebook about the television programmes in exercise C using the words below.

boring / quite good / interesting / funny / exciting / brilliant

I think westerns are brilliant.

Pronunciation

E
Listen to the sentences. Count the number of words.

1 [5] 2 [ ] 3 [ ] 4 [ ] 5 [ ] 6 [ ]

26

A
Use the words below and *did* to write questions.

1 what job / Butch Cassidy / do ?

   What job did Butch Cassidy do ?

2 Butch Cassidy / travel / a lot ?

   ....

   ....

3 what / Butch Cassidy / rob ?

   ....

   ....

4 where / Butch Cassidy and the Sundance Kid / go ?

   ....

   ....

5 the Bolivian Army / kill / Butch Cassidy ?

   ....

   ....

B
Now read the text and answer the questions in exercise A.

Butch Cassidy was a cowboy. He travelled around America with his cows. Life was hard – there were bears and wild cats. Many of the cows died when there was no water for them. Then, there was no work for Butch and other cowboys. Butch started to rob banks. One day he was in a saloon and he started to talk to a man. The man was called the Sundance Kid. They started to rob banks and trains with other cowboys. People called them 'The Wild Bunch'.

The sheriffs wanted to catch Butch Cassidy and his men. Butch and his friend, the Sundance Kid, decided to go to South America. They travelled to Bolivia, but they did not stop robbing banks.

People say that the Bolivian army killed Butch Cassidy and the Sundance Kid. But Butch escaped and travelled again to the United States. No one knows what happened to the Sundance Kid.

1 *He was a cowboy.* ....

2 ....

3 ....

   ....

4 ....

   ....

5 ....

27

A

Look at the title of the song. What kind of song do you think it is?

a) a children's song
b) love song
c) a song about cowboys

Listen and find out.

Oh! Susanna!

☐ a) The weather, it was dry,
☐ b) I'm going to Louisiana my true love to see,
☐ c) It rained all night the day I left,
[1] d) I come from Alabama with my banjo on my knee,
☐ e) The sun was hot and I froze to death,
☐ f) Susanna don't you cry.

Chorus

Oh! Susanna, oh! don't you cry for me,
I come from Alabama with my banjo on my knee.

B

Listen to the first part of the song again. Put the lines in the correct order.

C

How many rooms and house items can you find?

K	I	T	C	H	E	N
B	A	T	H	S	T	O
T	B	L	A	M	P	L
A	T	O	I	L	E	T
B	E	D	R	O	O	M
L	S	F	I	R	E	P
E	C	O	O	K	E	R

D

Answer these questions about your English.

1 When did you start to study English?

....

2 What was the name of your teacher?

....

3 Which book did you use?

....

4 Which activities did you like when you started?

....

5 Which activities did you dislike?

....

37

27

E

Read and listen to the story. Then read it again and answer these questions.

1 Where did John Dunbar go?

....

2 Which animal started to be his friend?

....

3 What did the Sioux call John?

....

4 Who did 'Dances with Wolves' marry?

....

5 What did the soldiers kill?

....

6 Why did 'Dances with Wolves' leave?

....

Dances with wolves

John Dunbar was a soldier in the US army. He travelled to the West to a fort. When he arrived there, there were no people at the fort.

John lived in the fort but he was not happy. He wanted to be with people. Then, a wolf started to come to the fort. After a time the wolf was his friend.

One day, some Sioux Indians arrived. They lived near the fort and John and the Sioux were friends. One day, John played with the wolf and the Sioux watched him. They called him 'Dances with Wolves'.

There was a white woman who lived with the Indians. John loved her and they married. He started to learn the Sioux language and hunted buffaloes with them. He liked the life of the Sioux and he liked the people.

One day American soldiers arrived at the fort. They killed John's horse and they wanted to take him to the East. The wolf followed him and the soldiers killed the wolf. But the Sioux attacked the soldiers and 'Dances with Wolves' escaped.

'Dances with Wolves' lived with the Sioux, but now he was not happy. He did not want the army to attack the Sioux. 'Dances with Wolves' and his wife decided to leave and live in the West. His Sioux friends were very sad.

28

Language revision

A
Complete the text with the past tense of these verbs.

arrive / attack / live / not have / kill / use

The Sioux Indians [1] *lived* on the plains of America. Then the white men [2] .... The buffalo hunters [3] .... all the buffaloes and the Sioux [4] .... any food to eat.

The Sioux did not want the white men in their land. Crazy Horse [5] .... the US Army at Little Big Horn and killed General Custer. Then the white men killed the great chief Sitting Bull and at Wounded Knee the soldiers [6] .... machine guns and killed three hundred men, women and children.

B
Use the words in the picture to write questions.

where what when

DID

you he she they

do go have watch

(on) TV? to school? to bed? (for) lunch? after school?

1 Where did she have lunch?

2 ....

3 ....

4 ....

5 ....

6 ....

39

28

Useful vocabulary
C
Look at these words from Module 4. Check that they are in your vocabulary book.

Nouns: house / dog / tent / clothes / buffalo / sheriff / cowboy / Indian / room / western / programme / cartoons / cooker / door / television

Verbs: travel / arrive / escape / return / study / learn / need / escape / talk / enjoy

Adjectives: comfortable / boring / interesting / exciting / funny / brilliant

Dr Grammar
D
Correct these mistakes.

1 Did you watch ~~to~~ television yesterday?

2 What did you studied?

3 Yesterday I visit a friend's house.

4 I did not studied English yesterday.

5 Did you enjoyed that film?

6 Yesterday I talk to a friend on the telephone.

Spelling corner
E
Underline the correct word.

1 They caried / <u>carried</u> their babies..

2 I travelled / traveled a lot.

3 They ussed / used buffalo meat.

4 Dogs pulled / puled their possessions.

5 She maried / married him.

Extra time!
F
Use the words in the diagram to write as many questions as you can about Butch Cassidy and the Sundance Kid.

Words in diagram: to South America / a lot / rob / catch / go / Butch Cassidy / travel / did / the sheriffs / The Sundance Kid / Butch and Sundance / work / escape / trains / banks / as a cowboy

1 <u>Did the sheriffs catch Butch and Sundance?</u>

2 ....

3 ....

4 ....

5 ....

6 ....

40

MODULE 5
TRAVEL 29

A
Read Paola's composition and correct the prepositions.

Paola Soares   Class 5B

I live (on) a small village near Viana do Castelo (at) Portugal. I get up (on) 7.30 (at) the morning and I leave home (on) 8.15. Then I go (in) foot to the village square. After that, I go to school in Viana (in) bus. (On) the afternoon, I come home (in) car, because my mum works in a shop (on) Viana.

(On) weekends (at) the summer and (at) the holidays I go to Viana (in) bicycle with my friends. We go to the beach. Sometimes I go with my mum and dad (in) car to the shops in Oporto.

B
Complete these notes about *you*.

Going to school

I leave home at ....

I go by / on ....

I arrive at ....

At the weekend

I go to ....

I go by / on ....

C
Use your notes to write a composition like Paola's in your notebook.

Language extra: the

| I go to **the** beach / cinema / shops / disco. |
| I go to bed / school.   I go home. |

D
Complete these sentences with *the* or –.

1 On Saturdays I go to .....**the**..... cinema.

2 I don't go to .... school on Sundays.

3 I go .... home at 5 o'clock.

4 We go to .... beach to play.

5 My sister goes to .... bed at 8 o'clock.

E
Write the days of the week in order.

Wednesday / Monday / Sunday / Thursday / Tuesday / Saturday / Friday

1 Monday   2 ....   3 ....

4 ....   5 ....   6 ....

7 ....

Listen and check your answers. Which days of the week do you like and which do you dislike? Complete the faces for the days.

Like = ☺   Dislike = ☹

41

30

A
Listen to the conversation and complete the times.

Fun Day in Central Park!

.... a.m.	leave the hotel
.... a.m.	visit the zoo
.... a.m.	sail a boat on the lake
.... p.m.	hamburger lunch
.... p.m.	watch a puppet theatre
.... p.m.	see a skateboarding competition
.... p.m.	watch a firework display

Language extra: Times

a.m. = after midnight / in the morning up to midday
p.m. = in the afternoon / in the evening up to midnight

B
Listen and write the times in numbers, using *a.m.* or *p.m.*

1 2.15 p.m.
2 ....
3 ....
4 ....
5 ....
6 ....

C
Write these times in words.

1 3.45 p.m.
   Quarter to four in the afternoon

2 9.00 a.m.
   ....

3 6.00 p.m.
   ....

4 1.15 p.m.
   ....

5 10.30 p.m.
   ....

6 11.15 a.m.
   ....

D
Invent a 'Fun Day' for your town. Write three times and sentences.

Fun day in ....

1 10.30 a.m. visit the computer game shop

2 ....

3 ....

4 ....

31

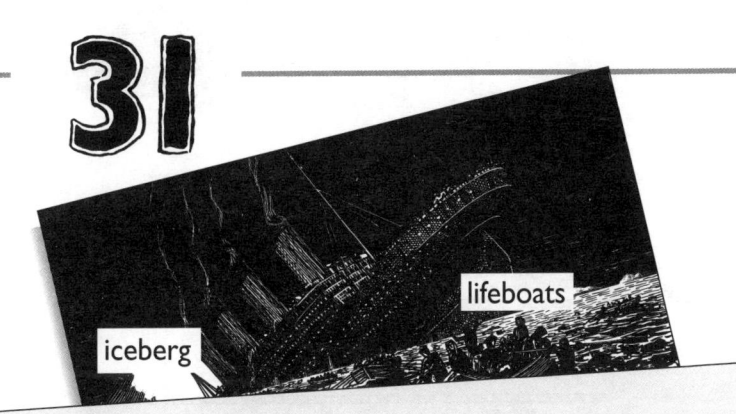

The Titanic

A British company ¹ _made_ the Titanic, an enormous passenger ship. On 10th April 1912 the Titanic ² _____ Britain to cross the Atlantic. It ³ _____ 2,227 passengers.

There ⁴ _____ many rich and famous passengers on the ship. They ⁵ _____ in first class seats and ⁶ _____ and ⁷ _____ in the first class dining room. In the evenings they ⁸ _____ to music and ⁹ _____ .

The poor passengers ¹⁰ _____ their meals in the third class dining room. They ¹¹ _____ a lounge and they ¹² _____ in uncomfortable cabins.

On the night of 14th April the Titanic hit an iceberg. Some of the women and children ¹³ _____ in the lifeboats, but many people stayed on the ship. The orchestra ¹⁴ _____ playing! Finally the Titanic sank at 2.20a.m. on 15th April, and many people ¹⁵ _____ .

A
Complete the text above with the past tense of these verbs.

drink / escape / listen / die / dance / to be / sit / have / not have / leave / eat / make / not stop / sleep / eat

B
Listen to the story of The Titanic and check your answers to exercise A.

C
Write six sentences in your notebook about what *you* did yesterday. Use these verbs:

get up / drink / eat / go / have lunch / leave

1 I got up at eight o'clock.

Spelling corner
D
Number the months of the year in order.

August ☐   December ☐
February ☐   June ☐
May ☐   April ☐
November ☐   January ☐
July ☐   September ☐
March ☐   October ☐

Language extra: Dates

Write: On 10th April
Say: On the tenth of April

E
Write four important dates for *you*.

1 My birthday = ...
2 ....
3 ....
4 ....

32

A
Read about Sarah's life. Then listen and find four things that are *not* correct in her composition.

READING
1 She was born in 1982.
2 Her sister was born in 1985.
3 She went to Cyprus in 1989.
4 She went to Spain in 1991.

LISTENING
1 She was born in 1981.
2 ....
3 ....
4 ....

Early memories

I was born in 1982 in London. My sister Anna was born in 1985 and we moved to a new house. The house is near the river. In 1986 I went to a small school. The school was called East Sheen Primary School. I had a very good teacher. The teacher was called Mrs Evans.

In 1989 we went to Cyprus on holiday. We stayed in a hotel. The hotel was near the sea. Then in 1991 we went on holiday to Spain. We stayed in a villa. The villa was fantastic and there was a swimming pool. The pool was enormous and we swam in it every day!

(1)
(5)
(10)
(15)
(20)

Language extra: a / the

> We moved to **a** new house.
> **The** house is near the river.

B
Look at the notes below. Write a description for each note from Sarah's composition.

1 a new house (line 4)
   The house is near the river.
2 a small school (line 6)
   The school was called East Sheen primary.
3 a very good teacher (line 9)
   ....
4 a hotel (line 13)
   ....
5 a villa (line 16)
   ....

C
Write about *your* early memories in your notebooks. Use Sarah's composition as an example.

D
Circle the odd-one-out.

1 car   bus   (bicycle)
2 ship   airship   aeroplane
3 on skis   by car   on foot
4 bicycle   horse   elephant
5 Monday   April   Wednesday
6 summer   May   June

33

A
Janine and Will are camping. Complete their dialogue using the words below.

is / isn't / are / aren't

JANINE: We need to go to the supermarket. What have we got?

WILL: I don't know. Ah yes! There ¹..*are*.. some crisps.

JANINE: ² .... there any bread?

WILL: No, there ³............ any bread. And there ⁴............ any orange juice either.

JANINE: ⁵............ there any bananas?

WILL: Yes, there ⁶............ some bananas, but there ⁷............ any apples.

JANINE: What about water? ⁸............ there any water?

WILL: Yes, there ⁹............ There ¹⁰............ four bottles.

B
Listen to the dialogue and check your answers.

Language extra: How many...?

How many oranges are there?
There are three oranges.

C
Write questions and answers about the things in the picture in exercise A.

1 (packets of crisps)
   How many packets of crisps are there?
   There are two packets of crisps.

2 (oranges)
   ....
   ....

3 (cans of cola)
   ....
   ....

4 (bananas)
   ....
   ....

5 (bottles of mineral water)
   ....
   ....

D
What are these words?

1 rotscar *carrots*   4 eseche ....
2 ngesora ....   5 akesc ....
3 adbre   ....   6 plesap ....

E
Write about the food in exercise D in your notebook. Which do you like? Which don't you like?

I like apples but I don't like carrots.

45

34

A

Read and listen to the story of Ulysses. Write the titles of the paragraphs in the correct place in the story.

- Arriving in Ithaca
- The Sirens
- Circe and her magic
- Scylla
- The Cyclops
- Leaving Troy

B

Read the story again. True or false?

1. Ulysses was from Troy. **F**
2. The Cyclops had one eye. ☐
3. Ulysses and his men used cows to escape from the Cyclops. ☐
4. Circe was a horrible monster. ☐
5. Ulysses listened to the Sirens' songs. ☐
6. Scylla killed six of the men. ☐
7. Ulysses and all his men arrived home. ☐

The Story of Ulysses

1 Leaving Troy

Once upon a time there was a man called Ulysses. He was from Ithaca in Greece but he travelled for many years. One day he decided to return home. He left the city of Troy with his men and he sailed west.

2 _____

After some time they arrived at an island. They stopped to get food and water. On the island they saw a monster, a terrible Cyclops with one eye. The Cyclops took Ulysses to its home and ate two of his men! Ulysses wanted to escape. When the Cyclops slept, Ulysses put his sword into the monster's eye. In the morning, Ulysses and his men used the Cyclops' sheep to escape.

3 _____

Then Ulysses came to another island. There was a beautiful woman there called Circe, but she used magic and changed the men into pigs. Ulysses had a magic plant and he did not become a pig. Finally, Circe changed the pigs into men again and Ulysses sailed away.

4

After that, Ulysses and his men sailed near another island where there were women like birds called Sirens. The Sirens sang beautiful songs. People wanted to listen to the songs and their ships went onto the rocks and sank. But Ulysses covered his men's ears and they did not hear the songs. Ulysses wanted to listen and his men tied him to the ship.

5

Next Ulysses' ship came to a place where there was an island on the left and a dangerous whirlpool on the right. On the island there was a horrible monster called Scylla. She killed six of Ulysses' men but the ship escaped.

6

Finally there was a terrible storm - the weather was very bad. The ship sank but Ulysses was lucky and he escaped. He swam for a long time and met some friendly people. Ulysses returned in one of their ships to his home in Ithaca.

35

Language revision

A

Use the notes below to write about Angela's visit to London. Put the verbs in the past tense.

1 get up / 6.30a.m. / have breakfast
   I got up at half past six and had breakfast.

2 leave home / 7.00 / take bus / railway station
   ....

3 go / train / London / arrive / 10.04
   ....

4 morning / see / the Tower of London.
   ....

5 have lunch / near the Tower of London : eat sandwiches / drink orange
   ....

6 afternoon / go boat / on the River Thames / to Greenwich
   ....

7 go to cinema / bus / see a western
   ....

8 come home / 11.00p.m. / go to bed
   ....

B

Put these words from Module 5 into the correct column.

water / bicycle / hydrogen gas / hair / snow / people / cow / salmon / bread / cheese / apple / rice / lemonade / crisps / sandwich / hamburger

Countable	Uncountable
bicycle	water

Useful vocabulary

C

Check that these words are in your vocabulary book.

bus [TR]   ski [V]   leave ☐   boat ☐
night [T]   afternoon ☐   ship ☐
come to ☐   get on ☐   return ☐
winter ☐   morning ☐   bread ☐
rice ☐   chicken ☐   train ☐
bicycle ☐   cheese ☐   tomato ☐
sugar ☐   arrive ☐   travel ☐
sail ☐   eggs ☐   carrots ☐
evening ☐   summer ☐   weekend ☐

Now put the words into the correct group. Transport (TR), Verbs of movement (V), Food (F), Time (T).

Pronunciation

D

Write the months in the correct column according to the stress pattern.

January / February / March / April / May / June / July / August / September / October / November / December

Group 1 = ■ □ □ □
January
....

Group 2 = □ ■ □
September
....

Group 3 = ■ □
....
....

Group 4 = □ ■
....
....

Group 5 = ■
....
....

Listen and check your answers. Listen again and repeat the months.

Dr Grammar

E

Correct the mistakes.

1 There is some people.
   There are some people.

2 Is there any sheep?
   ....

3 How many children is there?
   ....

4 There are some rice.
   ....

5 The people is not very happy.
   ....

6 Are there any icecream?
   ....

Spelling corner: ie/ee/ea/eo

F

Underline the correct word.

1 I leeve / lieve / <u>leave</u> home at 9.00a.m.

2 I go there at the weakend / weekend / wiekend.

3 Can you give me a piece / peece / peace of paper?

4 The peeple / people / peaple are in the bus.

5 There are lots of trees / tries / treas in the park.

6 There is a heeted / hieted / heated swimming pool.

7 Can I have a drink, pleese / please / pliese?

8 I really hate cheese / chease / chiese!

MODULE 6
PLANET EARTH

36

**ZORGON EARTH PROJECT:
HUMAN No 314**

NAME: Mark Wilson
AGE: 34 Earth years
HOME: Glasgow
JOB: Computer programmer
READS: Computer magazines
FOOD: Sandwiches/tea

A

Read the information about Mark Wilson and look at the photo of him on holiday now. Then complete the sentences with the correct form of the verb.

1 Mark (live) ......*lives*...... in Glasgow.

2 At the moment he (sit) .... near a swimming pool.

3 He usually (read) .... computer magazines but now he (read) .... a comic.

4 At the moment he (eat) .... a hamburger and he (drink) .... some lemonade.

5 For lunch at work, he usually (eat) .... a sandwich and he (drink) .... a cup of tea.

6 At the moment he (listen) .... to a cassette.

B
Answer these questions in full sentences.

1 What are you wearing now?
   I am wearing ....

2 What does your friend do at weekends?
   ....

3 What is your friend doing now?
   ....

4 What music does your teacher listen to?
   ....

5 What is your teacher doing now?
   ....

6 What are you doing now?
   ....

Spelling corner: Clothes
C

Here are some words, but with no vowels! What are they?

1 shrt =   4 shs =
   shirt
2 jckt =   5 scks =

3 trsrs =   6 drss =

50

37

A

Are these sentences true or false?

1 A thousand million people use some English every day. [T]
2 All computer information is in English. ☐
3 English is the language of Air Traffic Control. ☐
4 Half the world's letters and postcards are in English. ☐
5 You can read about Japanese news, in English, in Tokyo. ☐

Now read the text and check your answers.

A World Language: did you know?

- 1,000,000,000 people use some English every day!
- 80% of the world's computer information is in English.
- Half the world's telephones ring in English-speaking countries.
- An Italian pilot in an Italian aeroplane speaks to an Italian airport ... in English! 157 countries use English for Air Traffic Control.
- 75% of the world's letters and postcards are in English.
- Over half the world's 10,000 newspapers are in English!
- There are local English newspapers in Calcutta, Paris, Athens, Jerusalem, Cairo, Buenos Aires, Tokyo and Tehran.

Pronunciation

B

Number the languages and nationalities according to their stress pattern.

1 = □□☐   4 = □☐□□
2 = ☐□   5 = ☐□□
3 = □☐□

English ☐   Japanese [1]   American [4]
Indian ☐   Italian ☐   Canadian ☐
Spanish ☐   Arabic ☐   Portuguese ☐

Listen and check your answers.

Language extra: Farewells

| Bye!   See you! |

C

Complete these sentences.

1 .... tomorrow.
   Yeah, ...!
2 ...., Mrs Fox.

Listen and check your answers.

Which farewell is very friendly? ☐
Which is polite? ☐

Punctuation: Commas in numbers

D

Put commas in the numbers.

1 She earns £25,000 a year.
2 60000 people went to the match.
3 There are 850 pupils in my school.
4 Over 700000000 people speak English.

38

A
Write sentences in the speech bubbles.

1. Why ....?
   That's a good idea.

2. What about ....?
   OK, let's do that.

3. Let's ....
   No, thanks.

Now listen and check your answers.

B
Put the dialogue in the correct order. Then listen and check your answers.

A: Well, what about going to see Carol?

A: Oh, you're so boring!

A: OK, let's play a computer game.

A: Why don't we go to the park? [1]

B: No, I hate them. Let's do our English homework.

B: No, it closes at six o'clock.

B: No, she's doing her homework.

Spelling corner: Tricky ones
C
Look at the pictures and write the words.

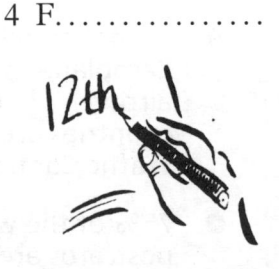

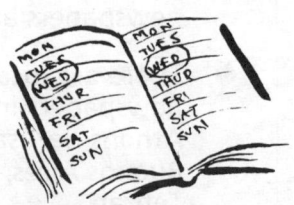

1 s.................
2 c.................
3 b.................
4 F.................
5 t.................
6 W.................

39

A
Listen to the scientist. Where is she? Write 1, 2 or 3 in the correct box.

Polar region ☐   Hot desert ☐
Rainforest ☐

B
Listen to the first part again. Circle the animals you can hear.

parrots / monkeys / bears / insects / leopards

Language extra: the

> the Atlantic Ocean   the Himalayas
> the Nile   France   the USA   Everest

C
Put *the* or – in these sentences.

1 The airship crossed ..*the*.. Atlantic ocean.
2 We went to ....–.... France.
3 They climbed .... Everest.
4 I sailed down .... Mississippi.
5 She worked in .... UK.
6 They climbed .... Andes in .... Peru.
7 They sailed across .... Pacific to .... Japan.

Punctuation: Capital letters

D
Write the words which have a capital letter.

1 The capital of australia is canberra.
   Australia, Canberra
2 They climbed everest.
   ....
3 She sailed a boat down the river thames.
   ....
4 They travelled in the sahara desert.
   ....
5 We went to london on holiday.
   ....

Spelling corner: ar

E
Complete the sentences.

1 She went for a walk in the __ a r __.
2 I had a good time at your birthday __ a r __.
3 Zorgons have got four legs and four a r __.
4 Ask your __ a r __ __ __ __ questions.

Pronunciation

F
Listen. Are these words pronounced like *can* or *can't*?

	Like *can*	Like *can't*
1 hat	✓	
2 are		
3 dark		
4 thank		
5 sandwich		

53

40

A
Read the plans for a school visit to England. Write sentences about each day, using the words below and *going to*.

```
Summer trip to England

WED  am - arrive Heathrow
         Airport, London
     pm - train to Norwich

THUR horseriding

FRI  Cambridge visit
     CANCELLED

MON  local school-talk by
     headteacher about local
     history

TUES am - museum
     pm - cathedral
```

1 fly / London
   They are going to fly to London on Wednesday.

2 go by train / to Norwich
   They are going to go by train to Norwich on Wednesday afternoon.

3 not visit / Cambridge
   ....
   ....

4 a headteacher / talk / about local history
   ....
   ....

5 visit / a museum and a cathedral
   ....
   ....

B
What are you going to do this summer? Write five sentences in your notebook.

C
Match the parts of the words to make holiday activities.

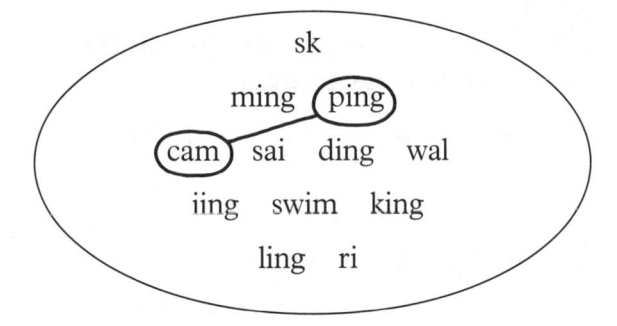

sk   ming ping
cam sai   ding wal
iing swim king
ling ri

1 *camping*   4 ....
2 .... 5 ....
3 .... 6 ....

Language extra: Wishes

| I want to . . . . |

D
Use the cues below and *want to* to write sentences about *you*.

1 (go to / a country)
   I want to go to China.

2 (meet / a famous person)
   ....

3 (visit / a city)
   ....

4 (be / a job)
   ....

5 (speak / a language well)
   ....

41

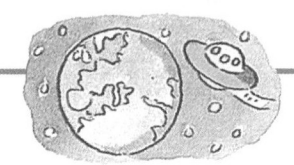

A
Read and listen to the story. Then answer the questions.

1 Write the names of the places in the first picture.

....

....

2 Was Ymir small?

....

3 What did Ymir drink?

....

4 Write names to complete the family tree.

Buri
|
Bor – ....
   |
┌──┴──┐
Odin ....

5 Did Odin and his brothers like Ymir?

....

6 What did Odin and his brothers use to make the world?

....

....

7 How did they make the mountains?

....

8 How did they make the first man and woman?

....

....

The Norse Creation Myth

Before there was a world, there was a cold place in the north called Niflheim. There was snow and ice here. In the south there was a hot place called Muspell. There was fire here. Between the cold and the hot place was Ginnungagap. There was nothing here.

Eleven rivers of ice went from the north to the south. The ice slowly changed to water and two animals came out of the water. One was a giant called Ymir, an enormous monster with hair of ice. The other was a big cow called Audumla. Ymir drank the cow's milk and Audumla ate the ice.

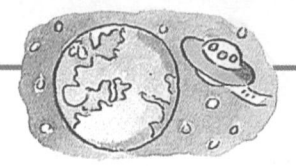

One day, the cow started to eat some ice and a strange person came out of the ice! He was called Buri. A long time passed. Buri had a son called Bor. Then Bor married Bestla and they had three sons - Odin, Vili and Ve. These were the first Viking gods.

Odin and his brothers didn't like the giant Ymir. They killed him and they used his body to make the world. First, they made the earth from his arms and legs. Next, they made the mountains from his teeth. Then, they made the sea from his blood. After that, they made the clouds from his hair. Finally, they made the sun and stars from some fire in Muspell.

One day, Odin and his brothers found two old trees. From these trees they made the first man and the first woman.

42

Language practice
A
Correct these sentences.

1 At the moment, she does her homework.
   At the moment, she is doing her homework.

2 He is practising his English every day.

3 Let's to play tennis.

4 I going to see the match tomorrow.

5 Why we not go to the cinema?

6 They go to visit the museum on Friday.

7 He is wearing school uniform every day.

8 At the moment he wears jeans and a t-shirt.

Useful vocabulary
B
Check you have got these words in your vocabulary book. Then put them in the correct column below.

shirt / nose / continent / cold / tropical / jeans / leg / jacket / head / ocean / hot / sunny / blouse / river / arm / mountain / rainy / snowy / capital

Parts of the body	Clothes
nose	shirt

Weather	Geography
	continent

Pronunciation
C
Put these words into the correct group, according to the sound of the letter 'o'.

Group 1 = clothes **Group 2** = body

nose [1]   continent [2]   cold [ ]
tropical [ ]   ocean [ ]   hot [ ]
snowy [ ]

Listen and check your answers.

57

42

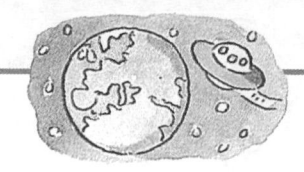

Dr Grammar

> They arrived **in** France / **in** London. ✓
> I arrived **at** the hotel / **at** the restaurant. ✓
> She arrived **to** school / **to** Germany. ✗

D

Put *in* or *at* in the gaps.

1 He arrived .... the station at 8 o'clock

2 The taxi arrived .... the airport late.

3 We're going to arrive .... Portugal soon.

4 They arrived .... school on a motorbike!

5 We arrived .... Paris at about 7.15.

Extra time!

E

Months quiz. Answer these questions.

1 In which month is your birthday?

....

2 Which are the summer months where you live?

....

3 Which month has three letters?

....

4 Which month has only 28 or 29 days?

....

5 In which month does your school year start?

....

F

Places quiz. Match the pictures below with the places. Write the letter in the correct box.

1 The Eiffel Tower, Paris. ☐

2 The Great Wall of China. ☐

3 The Golden Gate Bridge, San Francisco. ☐

4 Stonehenge, England. ☐

5 The Taj Mahal, India. ☐

6 The Pyramids, Egypt. ☐

Tapescripts

A Exercise D
1. Answer the questions.
2. Write a book quiz.
3. Listen to the story.
4. Match the titles with the pictures.
5. I don't understand.
6. Can you repeat that, please?

C Exercise C
1. My name's Sam Smith. Sam is S – A – M. Smith is S – M – I – T – H.
2. My name is Sue Simons. Sue is S – U – E. Simons is S – I – M – O – N – S.
3. My name is John Jones. John is J – O – H – N. Jones is J – O – N – E – S.
4. My name is Sarah Evans. Sarah is S – A – R – A – H. Evans is E – V – A – N – S.
5. My name is Peter Johnson. Peter is P – E – T – E – R. Johnson is J – O – H – N – S – O – N.
6. My name is Helen Mower. Helen is H – E – L – E – N. Mower is M – O – W – E – R.

1 Exercise A
1. My husband is a doctor and I'm a writer.
2. I'm married to Jackie. I'm a policeman.
3. My brother's name is William. My father's a policeman and my mother's a secretary.
4. I'm married with one child. My sister's name is Kathy and my brother's name is Robert.
5. I'm twenty-nine, I'm a doctor and I'm not married.

Exercise C
1. Robert's thirty-five.
2. Sarah's a doctor.
3. William's eight years old.
4. Jackie's a secretary.

3 Exercise A
INTERVIEWER: Tell us about things you've got at home, Frances.
FRANCES: Well, my favourite thing is my pet cat. She's called Kiki and she's lovely. I've got a bicycle, but it's a bit old.
INTERVIEWER: Have you got a computer, or computer games?
FRANCES: No, I'm not interested in computer games.
INTERVIEWER: What about English books?
FRANCES: No, I haven't got any books in English.
INTERVIEWER: And English music?
FRANCES: Yes, I've got a few music cassettes, pop music.
INTERVIEWER: Thank you, Frances.

5 Exercise D
1. He's a vampire.
2. He's from Transylvania.
3. My sister's got a cat.
4. My sister's tall.
5. It's got a big garden.

7 Exercise D
1 T 2 A 3 B 4 L 5 E 6 G 7 I 8 F
9 L 10 I 11 R 12 D

8 Exercise D

Group 1	Group 2	Group 3
books	coins	badges
stamps	models	boxes
comics	dolls	
	games	

9 Exercise D
1 woman 4 man
2 oxen 5 child
3 women 6 men

10 Exercise A
JASON: Look at this questionnaire. Can you swim, Sophie?
SOPHIE: Yes, I can. And you?
JASON: No, I can't. I don't like water! I can ride a bicycle. Can you?
SOPHIE: Yes, I can.
JASON: And can you ride a horse?
SOPHIE: No, I can't. Can you?
JASON: Yes, I can. And can you ski? I can't.
SOPHIE: Yes, I can.
JASON: Ah . . . I can't climb. Can you?
SOPHIE: No, I can't.

11 Exercise A
JASON: Do you like parties Alice?
ALICE: No, I hate them.
JASON: And your sister, Karen. Does she like them?
ALICE: Yes, she loves parties.
JASON: Oh? Does she like dancing?
ALICE: Yes, she does.
JASON: What music does she like?
ALICE: She likes Prince.
JASON: And who does Karen go to parties with?
ALICE: Look Jason. I don't know. Ask her!

Exercise E
1. Where do you live?
2. Does your brother like parties?
3. What music does he like?
4. Who do you dance with?

59

TAPESCRIPTS

12 Exercise A
1 In pairs, match the instructions with the pictures. Don't write in your book. Then listen and check your answers.
2 Look at the pictures and list your hobbies. In groups, read your list. Tell the class your favourite hobbies.

14 Exercise E
1 example   4 people
2 national   5 juggle
3 bicycle

15 Exercise D

Group 1	Group 2
shop	old
mosque	video
doctor's	local
olive	

17 Exercise A
JESSICA: My name is Jessica and I live in a small village in the USA. I like school a lot and my favourite lesson is Spanish. In my free time I listen to music – rock music. I listen to cassettes with my big sister.

PETER: My name is Peter. I live in a village in Scotland. I don't like school much. I suppose my favourite lesson is English. At home I like playing computer games – the Mario Brothers is my favourite game. I play computer games with my brother.

18 Exercise A
BRIAN: Hello, my name is Brian and my sister's name is Lucy. We've got new bicycles – mine is black and hers is white. Lucy collects dolls and I collect stamps. We've got two pets in our house – Eric, my dog and Tammie, Lucy's cat.

Exercise D
1 Good morning, Miss Thacker.
2 Hi, Laura!
3 Hi, Paul!

22 Exercise D

Group 1	Group 2	Group 3
played	cooked	carried

studied, talked, walked, arrived, liked, helped, travelled

24 Exercise C
TEACHER: Sam, you didn't do your homework! Why not?
SAM: Mmm, because I didn't have any time.
TEACHER: Come on. Where were you after school at 3 o'clock?
SAM: I was here at school. There was a football match.
TEACHER: And after that?
SAM: Well, at five o'clock I was at the supermarket with my dad. On Tuesdays we go to the supermarket to do the shopping.
TEACHER: And at 6 o'clock? Where were you?
SAM: I was at the doctor's.
TEACHER: Oh. And after that?
SAM: Well, it was my grandmother's birthday. I was at my grandma's house. She was 65.
TEACHER: And then?
SAM: We arrived home and then at 9 o'clock I was in bed!
TEACHER: Okay, I want it tomorrow!

25 Exercise A
PRESENTER: Today the subject of the quiz is The Wild West. Now, number one. A famous book about the American West is Little House near the Big Rivers. True or false?
GIRL: Er, I don't know . . .
PRESENTER: Correct! Number two. High noon is a famous western. True or false?
BOY: Er, I think it is . . .
PRESENTER: No, that's wrong. Number 3. The Mohawk Indians lived in Tipis. True or false?
GIRL: I think that's . . .
PRESENTER: Correct! Number four. Wyatt Earp, was sheriff of Chicago. True or false?
BOY: I think that's . . .
PRESENTER: Correct. Number five. The Plains Indians hunted buffaloes.
GIRL: That's definitely . . .
PRESENTER: Correct.

Exercise E
1 I think they're boring.
2 The nature programme was at eight o'clock.
3 There were two windows in the house.
4 I was in bed at nine o'clock on Sunday.
5 The house wasn't very big.
6 There was a small bedroom in the house.

27 Exercise A
I come from Alabama with my banjo on my knee.
I'm going to Louisiana my true love to see.
It rained all night the day I left.
The weather it was dry.
The sun was hot and I froze to death.
Susanna don't you cry.

CHORUS
Oh! Susanna, oh! don't you cry for me,
I come from Alabama with my banjo on my knee.

I had a dream the other night.
When everything was still,
I thought I saw Susanna
Coming down the hill.
A cake was in her mouth,
A tear was in her eye,

But I'm coming from the South,
So Susanna don't you cry.
CHORUS
Oh! Susanna, oh! don't you cry for me,
I've come from Alabama with my banjo on my knee!

30 Exercise A

GIRL 1: Hey, Sally look at this.
GIRL 2: Wow. Fantastic! A Fun Day in Central Park.
GIRL 1: You leave the hotel at nine o'clock in the morning. Then at half past nine you visit the zoo.
GIRL 2: Great.
GIRL 1: Then at half past eleven you go on a boat on the lake. And then you have an 'all American hamburger lunch' at one o'clock.
GIRL 2: And then at two you watch a puppet theatre. Brilliant.
GIRL 1: Mmm, and at four o'clock you see a skate-boarding competition.
GIRL 2: And in the evening at six you watch a firework display.
GIRL 1: I want to go on this Fun Day.
GIRL 2: Me too!

Exercise B

1 Two fifteen in the afternoon.
2 Six o'clock in the morning.
3 Eight thirty in the evening.
4 Ten forty-five at night.
5 Eleven fifteen in the morning.
6 Three forty five in the afternoon.

31 Exercise B

A British company made the Titanic, an enormous passenger ship. On the tenth of April 1912, the Titanic left Britain to cross the Atlantic. It had two thousand, two hundred and twenty-seven passengers.

There were many rich and famous passengers on the ship. They sat in first class seats and ate and drank in the first class dining room. In the evenings they listened to music and danced. The poor passengers ate their meals in the third class dining room. They didn't have a lounge and they slept in uncomfortable cabins.

On the night of the fourteenth of April the Titanic hit an iceberg. Some of the women and children escaped in the lifeboats, but many people stayed on the ship. The orchestra didn't stop playing! Finally the Titanic sank at 2.20a.m. on the 15th of April, and many people died.

32 Exercise A

I was born in 1981 in London. My sister Anna was born in 1986 and we moved to a new house. The house is near the river and we live there now. In 1986 I went to a small school. The school was called East Sheen Primary School. I had a very good teacher. The teacher was called Mrs Evans and she taught me how to read and write.

In 1988, I remember we went to Cyprus on holiday. We stayed in a hotel. The hotel was near the sea and it was very good. Then in 1990, I think, we went on holiday to Spain. We stayed in a villa. The villa was fantastic and there was a swimming pool. The pool was enormous and we swam in it every day!

33 Exercise B

JANINE: We need to go to the supermarket. What have we got?
WILL: I don't know. Ah yes! There are some crisps.
JANINE: Is there any bread?
WILL: No, there isn't any bread. And there isn't any orange juice either.
JANINE: And are there any bananas?
WILL: Yes, there are some bananas, but there aren't any apples.
JANINE: What about water? Is there any water?
WILL: Yes, there is. There are four bottles.

35 Exercise D

Group 1	Group 2	Group 3
January	September	April
February	October	August
	November	
	December	

Group 4	Group 5
July	March
	May
	June

37 Exercise B

Group 1	Group 2	Group 3
Japanese	English	Italian
Portuguese	Spanish	

Group 4	Group 5
American	Indian
Canadian	Arabic

Exercise C

PUPIL 1: See you tomorrow.
PUPIL 2: Yeah, see you!
PUPIL 2: Bye, Mrs Fox.

38 Exercise A

BOY 1: Why don't we play football?
BOY 2: That's a good idea.
GIRL 1: What about going for a hamburger?
GIRL 2: OK, let's do that.
BOY 1: Let's go to the cinema.
GIRL 1: No thanks.

Exercise B

A: Why don't we go to the park?
B: No, it closes at six o'clock.
A: Well, what about going to see Carol?
B: No, she's doing her homework.
A: OK, let's play a computer game.
B: No, I hate them. Let's do our English homework.
A: Oh, you're so boring!

TAPESCRIPTS

39 Exercise A

1 The colours are beautiful. Just look at that bird over there. But, my goodness, it's hot and very, very wet.
2 It's difficult to see, with the wind and the snow, but there is an Arctic fox over there, with its babies . . .
3 It is hot. Very, very hot. About fifty degrees. Or more. There's nothing in the sky. No clouds, no birds. Just a big, hot sun.

Exercise F

1 hat   4 thank
2 are   5 sandwich
3 dark

42 Exercise C

Group 1	**Group 2**
nose	continent
cold	tropical
ocean	hot
snowy	